For Tommy and Helen
with my love,
Rosemary

GW00601074

I am a field

Poems of place and nature

Rosemary McLeish

First published in 2019 by
Wordsmithery
5 Curzon Road
Chatham
Kent, ME4 5ST
www.wordsmithery.info

isbn 978-1-9160183-0-3
printed in Great Britain on recycled paper
by Inky Little Fingers

Cover artwork: Rosemary McLeish

This book is dedicated to

my brothers Martin and Richard,
fellow travellers
and to my husband, Richard Cooper,
faithful companion in good times and bad

Foreword

I grant indeed that fields and flocks have charms
For him that grazes or for him that farms;
But when amid such pleasing scenes I trace
The poor laborious natives of the place,
And see the mid-day sun, with fervid ray,
On their bare heads and dewy temples play;
While some with feebler heads and fainter hearts,
Deplore their fortune, yet sustain their parts:
Then shall I dare these real ills to hide
In tinsel trappings of poetic pride?

(From *The Village: Book I*
by George Crabbe, 1783)

After we moved to Kent eight years ago I thought I would like to try my hand at writing some nature poems. Although I had read much of the English tradition of "bucolic" poetry, I had never gone to the source, Virgil's *Eclogues*, so that's what I did first, in translation at least. I was surprised to discover that if this was nature poetry, I'd been writing it all along. Contrary to common belief, Virgil's *Eclogues* is not a bucolic idyll, not just a green thought in a green shade. He expresses as many concerns for the state of the world as anyone would today, contrasting a pastoral idyll with the harsh reality of country life. We all carry this idyll in our hearts, and I find I still do, even in the midst of complete disillusion.

I have twice lived in the country: once in the Trossachs for four years in a forestry village, and for the last eight years in Kent. Both times I expected to be soothed and uplifted by living closer to nature, and both times I discovered with shock that mankind's harsher, uglier characteristics show up far more in rural areas than they do in the concrete, litter and crowds of the city. It's a shock to discover that the beautiful loch on your doorstep is being polluted by sewage from the new holiday homes built on its shores in defiance of planning regulations by one builder with some sort of an in with the planning department. It is disturbing to discover that the field opposite your house has four crops a year and the necessary spraying gives you asthma, or that the foreign farm-workers who pick the fruit live on your doorstep in shameful old caravans let out to them at extortionate prices.

I find I cannot write about the beauty of the world, my greatest solace, without confronting the reality of its destruction with all the rage and sorrow it brings.

The book is divided into three sections with the loose themes of Innocence, Anger, and Sadness. These poems do not set out to be objective descriptions of nature or place. They are about my interaction with nature, and about my own nature. I have always been in love with the natural world, and feel so much part of it that these poems are where you will find me.

Rosemary McLeish, Selling, Jan 2019

Contents

i

Komorebi

The Japanese have a word
for my first wordless memory.
Helpless in my pram,
I gaze up at the sky,
delighting in the light
filtering through
flickering leaves,
tickling my eyes.
Just me and space,
no time or context.
It's the first time I begin
hazily to understand
there is an out there
and a me,
a being behind the eyes.

My first verb.
My first poem.

Chellow Dene

One blowy Monday in March
my friend Margaret takes me up
the long, puddled, disused drive,
past the untended rhododendrons,
away from the lodge house where
sheets flap on the washing line
and her Mum is making parkin,
scenting the warm old kitchen
with cinnamon and sugar.

I want to stop at the derelict
mansion house, to catch my breath,
peer in the ivy-covered windows,
imagine it, before it was a hospital,
peopled with a proper family, complete
with butler, housemaids, cook;
but she grabs my hand, pulls me
round the back, races me
through the unkempt coppice,
sidestepping the first pale shoots,
until, bursting out into the open air,
we are stopped in our tracks by
a sea of wild daffodils – wave after
wave breaking on the bare hillside.

I've already met Wordsworth, recited
that poem, reluctant, at a concert.
But now I see what he saw; and,
drunk with spring, go aeroplaning
down the hill, zigzagging around
the clumps spilling out of the grass.
Margaret follows, blue eyes laughing,
face red in the wind, blonde hair flying.

We pick until we can hold no more,
and still there are hundreds, thousands,
no space where ours came from;
we carry them down in precious armfuls,
careful not to drop a single one, to
Margaret's Mum, still in her pinnie,
who puts them in jam jars all along
the windowsills while we wash our hands.
We eat our warm parkin with milky tea
at the kitchen table, drink in the daffodils'
pale promise, exchange a grin.

The Colour of Water

The colour of water
has been a puzzle since
raindrops on the windowpane
first separated themselves from me:
bubbles on a flat plane
playing 'catch me if you can'.
Not red, as in ball
or green, as in grass
or blue, as in sky
(though sky in my eye
was not often blue).

The colour of water
is murky, muddy, blank
as my grandmother's eyes,
hidden, forbidden
as the canal, a surface
not to be broached.
Not red, as in simple
or blue, as in guileless
or green, as in gentle
(not even brown,
as in kind).

The colour of water
is fickle, false as the weather,
frail as friendship,
fragile as family bonds:
blue as the summer's day sea
red as the bridges in Kelvingrove Park
green as the pines at Kananaskis.
(One ruffle of wind
and it's gone).

The colour of water is grey
with a flickering of silver,
as grey as the ashes
we gave to the Wharfe, starting
their journey from Burnsall
to the slate-North Sea.
Not red, as in blood-clot
or blue, as in lips
or green, as in hearts
unused to grieving.

3

Water after rain is peat-brown
tanned as the tea Dad poured
in his saucer to cool.
Not blue, as in basilisk eyes
or red, as in hypertensive face
or green, as in larger than life.
I pour him into the cool
flow of the Kelvin,
which rushes the last of him
away from me.

Water in Peyto
is the greatest puzzle yet.
Never changing, grey skies or blue,
fringes of pine notwithstanding,
opaque, startling, still;
I will merge at my end
with its faraway depths –
Not red, as in ball
or blue, as in sky
or green, as in grass –
but turquoise,
as in me.

The turquoise colour of Peyto Lake, in the Canadian Rockies, is caused by the rock flora when the glacier which feeds the lake is melting in the summer. At other times of year it can be an intense blue.

Libellula

Today, I'm a dragonfly,
flitting over the calm green waters of my pool,
glinting irridescently in the sun,
but yesterday I rode on the wings of a hawk,
thrilled to the swoop for its prey.
I saw you, humans, like beetles crawling,
like shadows walking, lost in concrete.
I saw a mouse loom large as an elephant.
Its scream still rings in my ears.

Years of my life I spent lolling
like a cat on your sofa,
preening myself, licking my whiskers,
living (I believed) the life of Riley.

I'm not sure where I'll turn up next.
I'm tired of living...
I might be a book
lovingly fondled by kind hands,
or a crazy patchwork quilt
snuggling you warm in your bed.
I might be a washing line
braving the breeze in the garden,
a hair on your head
like a lemming about to fall off a cliff.
Maybe I'll take a ride on a sad grey mare,
all leather and jingling jangling bells.

I'm a nagual, an Ariel set free,
a will-o'-the wisp, a speck in the wind.
I'm a lally-gagger, a here-and-thereian,

Catch me if you can.

The Beanfield

The railway runs along the bottom of our garden
and if you go down to the station and cross the line
by the bridge, you come out bang in the beanfield.
If you take the path straight across and up, and
skirt around the spinney where the bluebells grow,
past our neighbour's orchard where the trees
grow old and crooked, past the poly-tunnels
and down the slope towards Boughton Oast,
you can be home in less than half an hour.

And in the spring when the blossom's out
and the bean flowers open their dark mouths
to marauding bees, when the sky is blue
and you're sitting in the garden, or driving
with the windows open down the lane, or
standing on the bridge listening to the cuckoo,
a hint of fragrance on a caress of a breeze
soothes the wrinkles from your brow, bows
to your still innocent heart, bids you join
in the celebration of beans, beautiful beans.

Happiness

I let it in for a minute,
my eyes open wide under a spring sky.
Then a breeze fluttered a page of my book,
losing me my place,
and my teeth clamped together again,
the furrow sharpened on my brow.

Later, another day,
it stayed for about ten minutes.
I'd gone to the part of the garden
hidden behind the rose trellis,
saw for the first time the rosa banksia
twinkling like fairy lights
in and out of the silver birch.

Well, we can't clap our hands
in sheer delight forever,
so I went back in to the washing-up
and remembered my aching back,
noticed how dirty the sink was,
how difficult the lime-scale to shift.

Yesterday it blind-sided me.
No late frost had killed the poppies;
the night's rain had only intensified
the honeysuckle's scent.
The garden was so loud with birdsong
I couldn't hear myself think
'this won't last, I'm not allowed'.

This afternoon, in this chair
under the blossoming hawthorn tree
I'm dawdling to my heart's content,
another dandelion clock
on the daisy-strewn lawn,
blithe as three years old again.

Ruffle my hair, little breeze,
little breeze,
blow me away.

That Girl

Was that her I glimpsed, turning the corner,
coat-tails flapping in the breeze,
sunspecs pushed to the top of her head,
a basket of flowers swinging in her hand?

I'm sure I know her – isn't she the one?
There she is, crossing the road, dodging
traffic, spilling crocuses on the centre strip.
Hurry, hurry, or she'll disappear again.

There she is, striding off towards the park,
lanky as a tulip, blonde hair flying,
gauzy green scarf floating in the breeze,
handing out violets to startled passers-by.

I know that girl. Didn't I see her only last year,
daffodil-pale, shivering down by the river?
Telling of shy shooting stars and dogwood,
Easter lilies nodding their heads in a graveyard?

And years ago, wasn't that her, making daisy
chains in the long, wet grass of the common,
holding a buttercup under my chin,
laughing at how much I love butter?

Look, she's there in the park, running ahead
under the frothy bloom of the almond trees,
flirty as the mallards on the pond, playing
hide and seek through the pussy-willow's fuzz.

I can't help it, I follow wherever she leads.
She's the one who whispered in my ear
in the playground "let's play kissing tig",
sent me, frisky as a lamb, into the lions' den.

Past Lives

I was a bitchy little burn, bubbling
down the hostile hillside,
wearing it away.
I was a secret waterfall.
I was the ferns growing by its side,
the slugs on the hidden path.
I was the slow-moving ocean,
the white-capped water, the turn of the tide.
I was urine, I was rain.

I was the mad wind, whipping the
cherry blossoms into drifts.
I was the haze on the horizon,
the shimmer of a hot day in Greece.
I was the eerie dance of the Northern lights,
the thunderclouds, the lightning flash.

I was smoke rising from a bonfire,
the crackle of the logs,
the flames licking and searing the flesh,
the charred choking stench
of the funeral pyre. I was the fire
erupting from the bowels of the earth.

I was the turned sod, the ploughed field,
the impenetrable mountains,
the everlasting plains.
I was the rock the house was built on,
and the sand.
I lay under tarmacadamed roads,
bearing the thundering traffic
and pushing up shoots and roots
on sidewalks and central reservations.

I was the wild rose and the fleabane,
the dandelion and the daisy,
the hot-house orchid, the orange blossom,
the tiger lily and the star of Bethlehem.
I was the rain forest, the bog,
the jungle and the desert.

I was the bee and the boll weevil,
the ladybird flying away home.
I was the swallow, snapping up gnats,
the crow scavenging road-kill.
I was the bloodlust of the lion,
the pack sense of the wolf,
the drudgery of the carthorse,
the lazy days of the cat.

Now I am the blood and guts of this creature,
the bone, the DNA, the connective tissue.
I whisper in the ear of her imagination.
I am an impediment in her eye,
lest she forget the crying game.
I poke her in the kidneys,
I tickle her nose.
I open her third eye;
a shutter clicks in her brain.
We are one.

No Shortage of Apple Pies

In the shade of an old, gnarled tree
small windfalls lie in clumps, all
higgledy-piggledy, dropped at the whim
of the wind or the weight of a branch.

They remind me of how apples used to be:
green, yellow, ochre, streaked with red,
patched brown with rot, worm-eaten,
raddled, every variation on round.

Scrumped from a local orchard, the best,
the juiciest, were always, as here
in this latter-day Eden, on the far
muddy side of the barbed wire fence.

These sorry specimens wouldn't make
the grade of the apple catwalk, but
who cares for the supermarket police
when these low lifes taste so sweet

and the Calvados of the mayor's wife
makes your eyes water as it snakes
down your throat like liquid fire,
essence of anarchy and apple pies.

Rhododendrons After Rain

Rhododendrons after rain
smell sweet, a little bit peppery,
but underneath that
a bitterness strikes a deeper note.
I'd forgotten that smell
until I moved back to Scotland,
renewed my acquaintance
with rhododendrons and rain.
It's the smell of home to me.
Now when I smell it
every day, I fall into
an earlier mode of being.
These days I dislike rain,
but that smell's as fresh
as the world's beginning.
It was there at my beginning,
at my first steps,
when I was it and it was me.

Rhododendrons after rain
mean feet planted in the earth,
and tumbling over giggling
into wet grass,
the world wheeling,
falling into my element,
hands muddy,
wide-eyed, enchanted,
avid for exploration.
Not my mother's daughter,
but free and fresh
and full of laughter.

I Dream of Mexico

In the Mexico of my dreams
I sit on the balcony
under a sizzling sky,
and the purple bougainvillea
against the blood red adobe
jumps to the rhythm
of a Spanish guitar.

Palm trees and prickly pears
lend a little green to the garden
but the sun beats down on me
and it's hot hot hot.
My Latin lover brings me
a screwdriver on the rocks
and naturally I am young again
and everything is easy.

I'll never grow old here,
never get up stiff and groaning
from this rattan chair,
to waddle through the cool house
and lie fanning myself,
feverish with heat,
in a darkened room.

In my dreams the beach
is only a thought away
and the azure sea makes
green patterns on the yellow sand.
The pace of life is all mañana
and I stick a hibiscus blossom
in my still-black hair and dance.

The sun scorches through me,
colours dazzle and assault me.
Slinky as a snake,
crazy as a Carnival Queen,
delirious as a dervish,
I, kaleidoscope, dance.

A breeze rattles the shutters
and flutters the curtains.
I shiver: and I am back in Glasgow
with a cooling hot water bottle,
a grey cat for company,
and an allergy to orange juice.

Nothing To Write Home About

Home is not where the heart's been broken,
home is in birthday balloons released
higher and higher into a bright blue sky.
Home is anywhere but here, under
the rhododendron bush, hiding in the
garden where thought should be taken,
not of the lilies toiling not nor spinning,
but of lupins in their infinite varieties,
poppies, deadly nightshade, foxgloves;
nor in the house, where there's bleach
in the mug on the draining board,
fire behind the fireguard, pills
in the bathroom cabinet, a razor
under the facecloth left in the sink.

I'm dreaming of escape in a hot air balloon,
getting lost, soaring out over the rooftops,
travelling far and fast in my need to break
out from the straitjacket of home.
But straitjackets are everywhere, joining
sleeves, flapping, dancing in the breeze,
singing "clap hands, here comes Rosie",
a Thursday's child travelling hopefully
but always arriving to disappointment
and the locked doors of an unsafe asylum.

There's respite at least on the common,
in buttercups held under chins,
in coltsfoot and long grass for crouching,
in wasting time and brains under
a mad-dog sun. Long grass that hides traps,
secretly rusting, waiting to ambush
an unwary foot. Dripping blood means
another trip to the white-coated hospital
in the old black leather pram, the locks
of the asylum snapping shut once again.

Walking in the cold wind of a grey day
among sand dunes at Wimereux, alone
in a bleak landscape, Houdini'd
from the quarrels in the van, the hugger-
mugger of the tent, the tedium of chores,
I am a balloon. I throw out the ballast,
let go the ropes, let the wind gust me over
the water. I am rising, higher and higher,
drifting farther and farther out. I am
unravelling into the sleeve of the sea.

I Want To Go There

I want to go there.
Even with my iffy indigestion,
hypertension, chronic pain.
Even though I can't walk far,
or uphill,
or carry much,
I want to go there.

I'll manage, with a grumble,
to adapt to
nowhere to sit down and rest,
outlandish bathroom arrangements,
heat, hairpin bends, caves.

Oh, I want to go there,
to the Europe of my youth,
when only flashes
of open-eyed surprise
pierced the dream
of styles in sandals,
of how do I look?,
of admiring glances from boys.

How outré, after dark and dismal home,
the colours of abroad, the light ...
The sun coming up, going down,
glittering morning,
bleaching noonday,
blinding afternoon.

Now I could really take it in,
fairy castles, gingerbread houses,
jewelled icons in
ancient dim churches.
The green gloom of 'La Venise Verte'.
Germans precision camping on the Lido;
cave dwellers a hundred miles from Madrid.
The rude watery jokes
in the archbishop's garden,
the Bridge of Sighs,
the miles and miles of Versailles.
Edelweiss growing on precipices,
oranges growing on trees.

Let's go there, you and I.
Never mind the fears, the failings.
Let's go there now,
before it's even more too late.
Even though I know it's gone,
lost in mass tourism's selfies,
I want to go there,
how much I want to go there!

Somewhere in the Netherlands, Summer 1957

Two men on motorbikes
riding through greenhouses,
the roar filling our eardrums
as they come closer and closer,
stop right next to our half-raised tent.
Helmets off, hair tousled, grins,
hands held out for a shake.

Two men on motorbikes
sharing their sausages,
drinking their Schnapps,
playing cards by lantern-light,
laughing, telling jokes,
rolling themselves up in their sleeping bags,
roaring off in the morning.

Dad says the Dutch are dealers in diamonds.
When I grow up
I'm going to marry a Dutchman.
I'll wear clogs and have blonde plaits,
a pushbike with a basket for my cat,
and a boat on the canal.
I'll plant tulips in my window box
and hang my bedding out the bedroom window.

I pretend it's for the diamonds,
for years,
but it's not.

They were so beautiful,
so bright-eyed and apple-cheeked,
so jolly, and so free.
They gave me a sip of their Schnapps,
and it warmed me all the way through.

We'll be grinning and singing all day,
my Dutchman on a motorbike and I,
we'll be camping in greenhouses,
we'll be laughing at the rain.

Philosophising in the Picos

This night of late dinner, long journey,
good companions, great cathedrals,
breathtaking landscapes and seventeen
thousand square metres of stained glass,
we went for a midnight stroll in the garden,
found glow-worms in the wall by the gate,
watched mist falling over the mountains.

Time, we think, goes slowly here.
How long does it take to cut and paste
seventeen thousand metres of stained glass?
Two centuries to build the cathedral –
the life's work of five generations.
The landscape's geological time
reduces our life-span to
a flea-bite on a sheep-dog's ear.
These mountain meadows, as flower-rich
as medieval 'mille fleur' tapestries,
took centuries of unchanging farming
to grow, yet could be destroyed
in the blink of an eye, the time
we took today to travel three hundred
kilometres – through villages with churches
intact after a millennium, where storks
return to their nests year after year –
flashing past hill-farmers scything their hay
with a boy, a tractor and two dogs.
Everything seems now and forever, yet is gone
in the seconds of short-term memory.

Why do we respond to ancient tradition,
to sitting looking at the view,
watching the cloud-pattern changes as
fascinating as a film; why does this sense
of the eternal enter us like balm?
It's the poem that's taken a lifetime,
and the time it takes to write it down.

Tormenta

Thunder bangs like a red wine headache;
sheet lightning blasts and blinds
like the sun shrieking through the shutters
the morning after a heavy night.
Here in Majorca God's not an old man
moving his furniture around in the sky,
he's a Glaswegian drunkard on a binge.

Dry river beds, gasping in the heat,
the imagination of water so far
from their dreams they don't remember
what thirst feels like, tremble as
the drunkard in the sky opens his britches
and pisses a torrent of pints of heavy
down their parched gullets, loses control
of his innards, spews out the remains
of a gargantuan curry and chips.

Gigantes

It was 45 degrees and people in Athens
were dying like flies. We thought we'd
get a cool breeze on a boat on the water
but sailed straight into the Libyan wind,
its breath on our faces like a hairdryer.
We stumbled back to the shade of our villa,
lay prostrate on our beds, unable to think
or even remember to drink, until the dark
night made it safe to go out. Frogs
croaked in their cisterns, bolted artichokes
creaked in the remains of the breeze,
the liquid night enfolded us.

We stopped for some food at a taverna
on the harbour, hotching with hungry
Greeks who saw nothing odd in dining
in the middle of the night. I felt funny –
cold shivers assailed me even as I dripped
with sweat. I thought I might faint, and
my head was a jumble as if I was dreaming.
There was a huge pan of what looked like
baked beans. The chef brought me over
a spoonful to try. Gigantes he called them.
I laughed, but they were. The bean that grew
into Jack's beanstalk. He saw me swaying,
said "Eat, eat!" and I did. Not after all
the Heinz variety, but something earthy
and soothing, a sort of a lullaby.
Mother Earth feeding her baby.
"Cook all day," he said, "twelve hours!"
And I ate them with horta pie from the hills,
and they were, as they say, to die for,
at 1 a.m. and 38 degrees.

Flight Time 8:04

Flight Time   8:04
Altitude   32,000 ft
Temp. outside   -71° F
Speed   684 mph

There's been nothing but sea,
an occasional rock...
now, ice is beginning.
And more ice,
gradually covering
patches of blue,
pools of green,
scratchings of rivers,
swirls and whorls
from the wind, the tide,
cross-hatchings of a
pen-and-ink drawing.

Now, again,
an empty page.
This time snow.
Endless, trackless, snow,
a down duvet stretching away
to unreachable horizons,
unfathomable,
waiting like a soft cold bed
for dreamless sleep.
Nothing.
No animal.
No plant.
No weather.
We seem to be standing still,
locked in a timeless universe
where blue sky and white snow
silently, seamlessly,
blend into each other.
Nothing to explore.
Nothing to catch the eye.
White fills the window.
I could vanish in it,
drown. ·

As if at the edge of the sea,
frozen waves fetch up on a frozen beach.
Ripples echo each other, subside.
A hidden tectonic shift, perhaps,
or some leviathan from the age of ice
shuddering in its sleep.

Like a knitted baby blanket,
snow drifts over bumpy ice,
All I can do is sit here
being carried over it,
unconnected –
this duvet, this baby blanket,
would kill me in an instant.
Nose hairs would freeze,
breath, marrow, bones.
I'd be one more stitch
in the meaningless waste.

Coming out of
the whiteness
at last,
into scrawls, blue holes,
grey admixture of shale,
the sediment of ages
like memory
filtering back after a coma,
we are flying over land again,
where we see the action of the ice
on sleeping giants of rocks,
nothing growing on them yet,

just the faint possibility
of moss, of grass, of leaf,
of landing.

Blossom Trees Dreaming

Mum's magnolia sheds half its petals
onto a flower-bed. Bedding plants
pop up pale blue and purple heads
from a pink and white pond,
water lilies in a painting by Monet.

The dogwoods' heraldic flowers,
green, cream, white, dotted so delicately
amongst the sparse leaves, turn the trees
into dancers in a ballet full of space
and froth, swaying gently in the breeze.

The triumphal arbutus shows off its
pale flowers as if to say: "You thought I
was magnificent, with my red trunk and
contorted branches, my dark green leaves
adding some colour to a winter's day,
but hey, look at these babies!".

Streets and streets of ornamental cherries
join branches in glittering arches
so pink and dense you can't see the sky;
and the fruit trees, in orchard gardens, white
and peachily frilly, the limes with their
drooping yellow flowerets like miniature
bunches of grapes, and all the variety
of exotic trees, put on their Sunday best as I
drive through the blue-skied mornings.

Although all this is as true as me sitting here
in this old armchair at the end of the day,
tomorrow I will walk down the nearest
"No Exit" street to the sea to feast my eyes
on the wild dark waves and the wild dark pines,
on the rocks and the herons,
the otters, the seals, the eagles –

and the blossom trees will be yesterday's dream,
forgotten like party dresses discarded on the beach.

My Blue Heaven

I've fallen in love with a flower.
(Don't look at me like that, it's true!)
I'm feeling all the usual symptoms –
damp palms, thumping heart, blushes,
thinking I've woken up in paradise.
Other people don't seem to notice
what I see in her, Camas Quamash,
my blue-violet heaven,
but all I know is, she's the one.

I don't remember our first meeting,
but I do know it was love at first sight.
Every year I come to see her, and this year
the spring was so late I thought
I'd missed her. When I saw her first buds,
I'm not ashamed to admit it, I cried.
Wouldn't you call that love?

Today in the meadows, I stumbled upon
a couple of rapt young lovers
where the intensity of the blue,
with its glints of royal and purple,
would knock anybody's knickers off.
Such a blue, as far as you could see.
The girl gave a heartfelt sigh.
"So many bluebells," she simpered.
"You certainly picked the spot",
I remarked, and the boy grinned.
Ho, ho, you've been here before,
I thought, but I didn't tell them

the real name of my secret love, she
who makes bluebells pale into the
insignificance of a humdrum marriage.
I won't tell them her life story, how
the first peoples planted her for food,
how Lewis & Clark mistook her blue for
lakes in the distance. I won't tell them
she's my soul-mate. I want to breathe
the world from inside her mouth,
smell her faint fresh oniony smell
as close as my sweat.
I want to taste her on my tongue.

I veer off by mistake into the water
meadows where the lupines will be next
to flower. I see the leaves and stalks
getting ready, but they can bloom in June
after I've gone – it doesn't matter to me.
My camas will be over by then, back
in the earth awaiting my arrival another
spring, and I returned to the rest of the year
of dandelions, pinks, nasturtiums, all the
common or garden flowers I married.

Visiting Victoria

We went for a walk in the morning
and the mist lay still on the water.
The dew silenced the grass as the deer
moved calmly through the gardens,
eating the new shoots of bluebells,
sniffing daffodils and moving on.

We went for a walk at noon
and the sun shone hot on our heads,
while we talked of the walks of childhood
and the meadows of poppies long gone.
A breeze riffled the sea where the otters
swim and the canoes turn around.

We went for a walk in the afternoon
and the sweat broke out on our backs
as we strode up the hill to the viewpoint
where mountains appeared, snowy white
above the hazy blue of the sea,
and two eagles disputed their territory.

We walked up Mount Doug in the evening,
watched showers of shooting stars falling,
and the hills like cut-outs in velvet
dreaming in the distance of summer,
and the world lay sleeping beneath us,
peaceful as seals in the sea.

We sat on the beach in the night
and our voices carried over the water.
We talked of people, here and departed,
of our lifetimes coming back to the Island.
And watched deer moving onto the headland
as a heron glided across the bay.

At Wickaninnish

Walking at Wickaninnish
in the clear sunny air
of this warm first day of March,
with not a soul in all the wide
expanse of beach but me,
my being stretches, shakes itself,
finds itself at home.
I come back here in spirit
when I can't sleep or the blues
gets hold of me; but now I'm
really here, it's the right place
and the right time and I'm
singing to myself a new song.
I've been asked to paint a grid,
embrace symmetry,
discard all I know of
colour, metaphor and things.
At first I see the pattern, the order,
the repetition, the reflection,
the very shellness of a shell.

But the shells along the tideline
are all broken. Sometimes
the sea is fierce and wild here,
and winter storms pound the
shells to sand. There are some
that are almost whole,
with just a small piece missing.
Some are old and worn,
some are young and soft;
some are cracked right through.
Sometimes it looks like new shell
has grown over old wounds, like skin;
sometimes the shell looks perfect
until you turn it over
and find its flaws,
striations like wrinkles,
barnacles encrusted like warts.

Some are embedded in others,
some joined like Siamese twins,
some have lost their other half.
Some are mere fragments
of what they were –
a bit of an ear,
a corner of a lip,
the iridescent mother-of-pearl
of the inside of a baby's mouth.
And then I see a perfect shell,
unmarked by the tides,
the idea made manifest –
the shellness that all shells aspire to.
Like snow, like sand, like logs,
like the ice in the canyon,
like curly hair;
how the universe loves to dance!

Before the roaring of the sea,
and the rolling of the waves,
I sing of the waves in the shells,
in the trees,
in the birds, in the air –
everything is a wave and a particle,
a symmetry in asymmetry.
I am me and a shell,
my cells are like shells
repeating, patterned, ordered,
the manifestation of the idea
of my DNA,
though I too am broken,
lop-sided, cracked.

Walking on the tideline,
I find a new thing:
an encrustation of shell-like matter.
Maybe it is a shell cancer.
Or maybe a shell began to make itself,
got broken, began again,
in its turn broken,
so the idea reincarnated itself,
failed to become perfect and began again,
until it became a cluster of shells,
barnacled onto each other,
each expressing the same
whorls and spirals, the same self,
the idea of reincarnation
incarnated in a shell.

I close my eyes
and the sound of the sea
is like a symphony,
like the music of the spheres,
like the Northern Lights
making their wild dance in the sky;
and in this ecstasy,
dancing in front of the booming sea,
I sing my new song
to the Queen of the Dance.

Hortus Conclusus

At the bottom of a rock-face –
the remains of a slate quarry
long disused – two abandoned
wheelbarrows rust in a neglected field.
Bolted sorrel and old dock leaves
sprout out of the thick grass,
brambles moulder on dying branches,
self-seeded trees interfere
with the beginnings of a wall.

Corrugated iron sheets cover
half the roof of the derelict house.
Broken downpipes lean wanly
against its rubbled remains.
Three orange plastic buckets add
a blob of colour by the new gate,
and a yellow one, like a faint echo,
lies on its side by the curious
concrete posts of what might once
have been a washing line.

Every blade of grass, every leaf,
stem, flower, is misted with a spray
of dew, forerunner of winter's frost,
and these plants, so familiar they
were written in the Book of Weeds
of my childhood – nettle, plantain,
groundsel, horsetail, vetch – will soon
be rimed and icicled with cold,
and crunch under Wellington boots.

Over a newly finished wall, a fiery
chestnut tree flickers in the breeze,
and one red leaf lies in the middle
of the field, blown there by a painter's breath.
The little oak tree seeded in the slate,
the smell of the chicken shit coming
from the earth, the charred remains
of a fire, could all be ghosts from the
bombed-out common of my youth,
except for the low roofs reaching
towards the ground, the mound of
old masonry rising up to reach them,
the blackbird's song breaking the silence.

Hortus Conclusus means enclosed garden. In the Middle Ages these gardens were
private spaces reserved for contemplative pastimes.

Night Watch

We wait in the car park
for the moon to come up
in the midnight-blue sky.
It bursts, as we watch,
out of the dark of the woods,
blooming from behind a cloud,
etching its edges in white light.

Now we can make out the trees,
and I see his fingers, thrusting
white out of fingerless gloves,
fumbling with the tripod,
dropping the lens cap, clumsy,
insensitive as doorknobs.

I stamp my feet in the background,
trying to keep warm, wondering
how long we will be here,
how many stars are up there,
whether the ring around the moon
means later there will be frost.

The moon moves on from the woods,
drifts behind the rim of the hill.
'Come on,' he says. 'It'll be over
the valley. It's all about the light.'
We stumble up the bumpy rise,
and I wait in the cold
as he sets up the tripod,
changes the lens, all thumbs;
the gloves don't seem to work.
'I think you need a hat,' I say,
tentative, not wanting to nag.

In the ball of the moon's madness
I read a possible future:
fingerless hands,
no more walks in the moonlight,
no more waiting for the dawn.
No more hunt, capture,
sharing of spoils.
But who cares about cold,
or circulation, or consequences,
when it's all about the light?
I shiver in the shadows,
holding the spare lens,
keeping the night watch.

Morepork and Moonless Night

We're at the farthest end of the world
and the farthest end of this country
as far from ourselves as we've ever been.

There are palms and ferns in the garden
and such a weariness inside. I wait
for the day's poem, but it doesn't come.

There are kiwi here, living wild,
we'll hear them in the night, we're told,
and I think of what animals would have

been here if our ancestors had been happy
with what they found and left well alone,
left all those sheep and cows at home.

I am so tired, so far from anything I know.
There's a morepork in the garden
and as I hear him cry "morepork, morepork,"

my mockery suspends. We walk twenty yards
from the house and we are surrounded
by stars, stars like I've never seen,

so close, we are in a bowl made by
a campsite and a circle of bush,
and the stars in the lid of the bowl

twinkle and twinkle their message
but I can't understand. As we watch,
heads reeling, we see a falling star.

A breath of something flutters my hair.
What do I wish? I wish I knew
the vastness outside as I wish I knew

the vastness inside, but both resist
my puny efforts at control. A poem,
a falling star, may come or may not.

An imaginary lion growls in the bushes,
I see two imaginary red tiger's eyes
glowing at us, but what is to fear?

Kiwis going about their business,
galaxies extending our horizons,
just us pukeko here, no worries.

Hoh

If I were a tree in the rain forest
I think I would raise my arms,
all forty-four of them, in hopeless
supplication to the far-off sky,
trying to reach the warmth, or at
least the light, from a watery sun.

When my skin grew scaly and flaky
from constant exposure to rain,
I'd be glad that sweaters of moss
came to clothe my naked limbs,
and shawls of lichen draped themselves
around my cold shoulders.

And after the lightning crashed
through the ruined ranks
of old friends and distant relations,
and a bolt of fire skewered me,
lopping bits of me off to die
on the forest floor, leaving me
diminished, helpless and alone,

I wouldn't care that the wind came
roaring through the ancestral halls
to knock me flying, uprooting me
from my bed of sedges and saprophytes,
crashing me to earth, bringing
saplings and other weaklings in my wake.

I'd look forward to becoming log,
becoming mulch, and I'd embrace you all –
lady fern, dwarf bramble, salal, salmonberry,
oxalis oregona, galium – I'd be proud
to have you seed on me, as I evolved
into loam, into food, into forest.

The Hoh Rainforest is in Washington State, USA, on the Olympic Peninsula.

Arum Lily

The stamen coming out
of the dark cleft, trembling
with pale yellow pollen,
is the tongue,
the tongue of the silky
white mouth waiting
to be kissed,
to be blessed
by another tongue exploring,
twining and twisting,
dropping its pollen
into the orifice
aching to be filled.

But there is no other.
The lily languishes,
beaten by the rain
in its corner by the shed,
unable to hide its
radiant white glow
against the ash-green
of the leaves, under
the evergreen creeper
on the crumbling grey wall.
It seems to be saying:

"Look at me, look at
my tears of rain,
my bruised edges.
Why have I been left
here by myself
like a child in the
naughty corner at school?
The things I could
say to you, the riches
I could spill into
your ear, your mouth,
the gentleness of
my velvet touch,
how I could enfold you,
how I could probe
to the very centre of you.

At least linger awhile,
consider me."

Bucolic

Driving along past the wheat field, the rapeseed,
the blue field of flax, we saw a sign just after
Frog's Bottom saying "Kent Cherries".
We turned off onto the muddy track through
an orchard of trees weeping to the ground
under the weight of ripe rain-washed cherries.
The track petered out in a clearing where a
jumble of old mattresses, fridges, car parts,
chairs, lay rotting in the long wet grass.

Out of a sagging caravan emerged a pretty,
dark-skinned woman with red lips and
kohl-rimmed eyes, and simultaneously
from a car up on blocks stumbled a fat,
fortyish man with a five-day stubble
and bleary eyes. He told us the van
had packed up early because of the weather,
suggested we came back tomorrow.

The woman, indifferent, went back in the
caravan, but the man saw the irony of
"no cherries today" in an orchard positively
groaning with them, and as we backed
the car to turn around, he reached up,
the gap between trousers and shirt increasing
to reveal a gut which had taken a fair amount
of years and beers to achieve its present hairy
perfection, picked a handful, thrust them at me
through the window with a gap-toothed grin.

Cherries never tasted so sweet or so English,
a mouth-watering memory from childhood:
fruit-pickers, a camp of travellers by the road,
ranging dogs, dirty washing on the line.
How I wanted to run away with the raggle-
taggle gypsies in those summer days of
picking blackberries in the disused quarry or
boiling up pick-your-own for next winter's jam.

As we drove home down the lanes,
Featherbed, Plum Pudding, all the Loves,
down Hogben's Hill, past the White Lion,
we knew that in this age of supermarket
cherries from Chile for Christmas, we'd had
our last encounter with midsummer magic.
The next year, they didn't come again.

ii

I am a Field

I am a field,
flushing as the late summer sun
burnishes my golden stubble.

Listen, I don't want your raptures.
It's only a trick of the light.
To tell the truth, I am very tired,
and inclined to snap,
to bicker over trifles,
remembering the clatter and batter
of the overnight harvester
keeping me from my rest.

What used to take
three men and a boy
two weeks of solid work
in the Indian summer sun –
days of jokes, rivalry, beer –
a peaceful slow harvesting,
like a gentle massage,
very soothing to the soul –
now brings new meaning
to phrases such as
riding rough-shod
and getting a good seeing-to.

I am a field.
Tomorrow or the next day
I will be stinking.
People passing will hold their noses,
turn their faces away from me,
as I flinch and itch
and blush with shame
at the filthy chemicals
you have sprayed on me.

Before I know it,
in the fog of October
or the frosty moonlight of November,
you will come in the night
and ravish me with your
rattling machinery again.
Three hours on the spreader,
three hours on the sower,
three hours on the harvester,
job done.

No more haystacks,
no more gleaning,
no more harvest home.

I am growing into
a clapped-out old woman;
and I am angry.
I never complained before
and now you won't listen.
You want to wring every last ounce
out of me, keep me fertile
long past my use-by date.

I am a field.
I used to be home to flowers and bees,
I sheltered small animals,
gave delight to sunburnt farmgirls
drowsing in the buzzing noontimes
amid the chitter-chatter of birds.
I've had it with all of you humans
and your shenanigans.
I wish the wind would get up,
blow as hard as it can,
and scatter my sorry soil
into the atmosphere,
so nothing will grow on me,
nothing will feed you,
and you will find out
that all worlds, including yours,
come to an end.

Till all the seas gang dry

Autumn used to smell of bonfires
in people's back gardens, damp
wood and wet leaves smouldering,
smoke mingling far enough away
to conjure up cosy scenes instead of
spells of wheezing and coughing.

But now the smell of smoke comes
from burnt offerings on summer
barbecues, our neighbours have
artificial grass and paving stones
and a palm tree, no pruning required,
leaf fall not an issue. The year

slides imperceptibly into winter,
the red, red rose blooms all year round,
the trees blossom out of the calendar.
Sometimes it seems the earth's akilter,
the seasons only fodder for nostalgia.

We've slipped our moorings from
the sun and moon, the seas have near
as nonsense run dry, the trees might as
well be bread and cheese, the icebergs
are melting wi' the sun, my dear, and
we're running crazy in a world not of
paper and ink but plastic and fake news.

Future Imperfect

Our granddad told us there used to be
things called roads that people got about on,
not like us, walking, but sitting in machines
which went so fast you could get to a
faraway place in a day! Mum rolled her eyes
as usual, and when I said what's a place
he got flustered and said don't be silly,
somewhere else, isn't it? We didn't believe him.
Mum says all that generation are sun-addled.
Got burnt potatoes for brains. That made us laugh,
but I thought I wish I had a potato right now
and I wouldn't mind at all if it was burnt.

Remember that old woman from across
the marsh? She told us it used to be a garden
full of beautiful flowers in every bright colour,
not just brown and grey like it is today.
I think they tell us their dreams, or how they
would like the world to be. I know they talk
about the sun as if we should be glad of it,
but we are people of the wet, my brother and I,
and anyone who joins our gang has to abide
by the rules of rain. Mum says we don't know
how lucky we are that she survived the droughts
and fires and walked across the desert to the
salt marsh, till her feet were blistered raw,
and her eyes forever dimmed by the cruel light,
and we must never forget to perform the rain
dance and make sure to follow the correct
procedures and above all we must have
nothing to do with the people of the sun.

A New Fashion in Stilts

The electricity's off, the gas is kaput.
We've used all the oil, both crude and refined.
The fish in the sea are all cod, dead cod.
The prairies are bogs so we've got no bread,
can't even eat cake.

We make our homes on the roofs of houses,
on the spires of churches and the tops of high trees,
looking down on pools, reservoirs, tarns, floods.
Cycleways are rivers, motorways twin canals.
Horses can swim now and
cows climb trees.

We are learning new trades – flotsammers
and jetsammers, floggers and keepers,
bodgers and scroungers.
Dowsers are dead as dodos,
boatbuilding's the new motown,
roofers are kings.

Leaf and resin raincoats are this season's black;
everyone's auntie's an umbrella designer,
wellingtons all the rage. The hairy amongst us
grow it long for warmth,
though we're OK for rugs,
dead sheep common as toads.

The water lies still, silent under a sailing moon.
The earth turns once again
in its blind orbit round the sun,
settles into the Aquatic Age.
Water thieves crouch
like rats in the rushes.

Second Arkists hold secret meetings,
evangelicals pray to Neptune,
Old Agers to Astarte,
fat cats do black market deals in the darkness.
Politicians, those cheaters, exhort us
all to pull together,
all stroke together –
if we all splash together,
we'll row their boat home.

Old Buffalo

Old Buffalo wakes up in the morning,
creaks to his arthritic knees, groans as he
lumbers to his feet, looks about him,
dopey with sleep, confused. Where is he?
Instead of the herd, he sees a long string
of something he doesn't know how to
think about: horses, he knows them
from the past, and those strange creatures
which stand up on their hind legs and
make a lot of noise, he's seen them before.
But what are those huge lumbering things,
moving head to tail across the prairie?
Time was, when his eyes were still good,
he could look across the world and all
he would see was food, mile upon mile
of delicious food, swaying in the breeze,
glinting in the sun. But now everything
is changing, he doesn't understand the
barren patches, and where is the herd?
There used to be buffalo everywhere,
eating, and when he was king, cows
for the taking, sons and battles and glory.
Now he sees the last of them, so few,
moving away in the distance, leaving him,
the sign that his time has come. Behind
his back in the night he's been ousted.
He bellows and stamps but he's tired,
he's finished. They don't look round.

He thinks he'll go to the buffalo jump,
take the hero's last leap, but on the way
death comes to meet him, in the guise of
a greedy little man on a pony with a rifle,
who has no use after all for the worthless hide,
the mangy hump, or the withered old balls.

Glen Fruin

We're so used to the pylons our eyes unconsciously
subtract them from the landscape, still green
on this bright winter's day, the slanting sun
lending a false promise of warmth outside the car.
Sheep huddle by hedges, in pens, splotched with
sky-blue, lime-green, hot pink paint, bizarre
in this bucolic glen. One flock dyed the bronze
of bracken look like a new breed, at least fit
more naturally in the scene. Bracken, I recall,
is an intruder here, and I wonder what other
invaders colonised through the years. Certainly
the stands of pine; but was this always boggy,
springy ground, with short turf, sedges, iris?

Two lines of hills mark the limits of the glen,
and we feel a great peacefulness, enclosed
in the landscape's arms, as if time stretched
out before and behind. Only one or two white
houses half hidden in evergreens, otherwise
sky, sheeptorn grass, the one empty road.
I notice in the midst of this flat plain a strange,
squarish hill, almost artificial, wonder
if it's a barrow or an iron-age fort remains.
We're not far from Glen Douglas, perhaps
it's a rogue arms cache, says my cynical friend.

We haven't been to Glen Douglas in twenty years.
but the Glen Douglas story still drops like a stone.
Walking from Arrochar through the glen,
my legs gave out after five or so miles
(a warning of the M.E. that's kept me away
from glens since then), and I lay on the ground,
unable to walk the extra mile to Inverbeg.
Out of nowhere appeared a little white dog,
who tugged at my coat, and tugged and tugged
until I got up and followed him, only leaving us
when we got to the road and the bus stop.
That exhaustion was surely a reaction to
this our first, terrible walk – finding myself
walking through an arsenal not on any map,
not in any memory. Maybe that's when
defeat and despair entered my soul
and Scotland became a toxic place to me.

If there is a landscape left in 2,000 years,
maybe some archaeologist will come across this
bunker, and think how odd, perhaps it is
a more recent religious artefact akin to those
found in Kilmartin glen. Perhaps he'll start
a whole theory about the spread of people
from Argyll. Finding no record in official
documents, he'll direct his students to start
digging, hoping for a cache of buried jewels –
blow the whole of Scotland to Kingdom come.

I don't know about nuclear weapons and what
would detonate them. Perhaps the floods and
avalanches of global warming will have done
their work, set off this whole arsenal in 2050
or thereabouts; and there will be no landscape,
no bunkers, no archaeologist. I remember now
how, in the fifties, sixties, we ridiculed an Aunt
for refusing to visit Loch Lomond because
her beloved hills were riddled with nuclear arms;
but already, Loch Long had been used for
torpedo practice, and anthrax dwelt in the
Highlands even as I made mud pies as a wee girl
in Westerton, worrying that danger lay in the
cottages on the other side of the canal.

We come out of Glen Fruin to that glorious view
of the Loch and the mountains, today so still
it's as if frozen in time, and I feel that old
helplessness creep up on me. What's the point
of writing poems, of casting votes, that make
no earthly difference? We pass the little tinpot
castles of retirement homes, the pitiful remnants
of the Faslane caravans, the buoys dotted about
on the loch, the boats put up for winter in the marina,
all a reflection of someone's country of the mind.

We don't come this way very often any more –
once in a full moon rising at the point of the
setting sun – how could we live, otherwise?
How get over the years and years of M.E.?
We join the rest of the myopic, not mentioning
the herds of elephants trampling down
the west coast of Scotland, telling visitors how
beautiful it is, what a wilderness, what peace.
I look at it all through sore eyes that need
artificial tears these days, dried up
as they are from too much crying.

Red Rebecca *(A song of the Hebrides)*

That black pig McLeod
shat in my water.
All my bairns drank it.
It was the death of my daughter.

My wee white hen Camille
strayed over on his croft.
He took to her with a hatchet.
No more eggs in my hen loft.

They call me Red Rebecca
because I'm consumed with rage.
I do my work, I tend the beasts.
Forgiveness I cannae manage.

That long streak of piss McIver
took the books with me on Monday.
Down on his knobbly knees on the floor
as if I didnae keep the kirk on Sunday.

Praying to scare the Red from me!
He's away with a flea in his ear
(as well as mud, and worse, on his trousers)
to give McLeod a taste of the fear.

My milking coo took sick and died
and I just knew who it was killed her,
black-hearted heathen that he is
and wicked his tongue that felled her.

I'd eaten poor headless Camille
and I buried my daughter that died.
When I gutted fair Elspeth the coo
that was the day I cried.

My man told me to haud my wheesht!
What with him in a constant gloom,
Piety McIver wringing his hands
and old Mad Margaret prophesying doom,

I saw red. I SAW RED. Went haring up the hill
swinging my new whetted cleavers
and in his filthy midden of a hoose
I sliced that pig into rashers.

Floor awash, walls spattered,
myself dyed red with his blood,
they call me Red Rebecca
because I did for that pig McLeod.

The Minister wailing and weeping
thundering out warnings of Hell
turned the whole kirk against me
with a Shunning: candle, book and bell.

But I don't give a rat's arse about them,
I'm for an orgy of hating,
watching black McLeod on a spit
turning and turning to bacon.

They call me Red Rebecca
for the flames of Hell – as if they matter.
The one thing I know is: anything's better
than that black pig McLeod's
shit in my water.

In a Hebridean village the crofts were often placed one above the other by the side of a burn which provided them with water. Children died of typhoid because they drank water fouled by people who lived further up the hill.

The reference to the Minister is to the Wee Frees, an extreme Protestant sect which converted the islands in the 19th century.

The blackhouses accommodated both people and animals with only a flimsy partition between them.

Mystic Beach

We emerge from the rainforest onto
a deserted beach. A double waterfall
cascades over the lip of a sandstone scarp.
We wend our way around and over
salt-bleached logs, floated down
from the clearcut up north.

Buoys which could be whales
and buoys which could be seals
distract us from a family of otters
playing fearlessly around a rock
by the tideline. A drift of mist

turns the mountain view across
the straits into a Chinese painting.
In the west, where the mountains
open out to the sea, the sun slants
its beams low over the horizon.

We are alone on a deserted beach,
five of us, all in our varying states
of loss and loneliness. I remember
the first time I came to this coast,
longing for a soul-mate to share it.

With the unseen whales and seals,
the barely noticed seagulls flying by
on their wave of salt-water chat,
this empty landscape is as crowded
today as a First Nations print of
ancestral faces in waves and clouds.

They are all here, the ex-wives,
the darling who died, brothers
elsewhere, brothers dead;
the family we met in the carpark,
their left-behind pueblo shrines;
our companions from other times.
This ancient seascape holds us all.

Clair de Lune

Hers is the last house in the village.
She wakes at 2 a.m.,
the bed empty beside her.

She thinks he'll be in the
bathroom, or losing
his way back, wandering out
in the dark, looking for
a glass of whisky.

Then she remembers:
the space in the bed is
permanent now. Tears, her
only night-time companions,
slide unheeded down her cheeks.

Roaming through the house,
she sees the moon over the loch.
A slight touch of mist, otherwise
clear sky. And what a moon!
Its light, clear as day, lends
enchantment to the trees,
the bowl of hills,
the newly maple-less garden;
pours in, cool as water,
through the uncurtained windows.

She could walk into the woods,
into the night, walk and walk,
let the moon bathe her white hair,
her wet, ghost-like face.

An Old, Old Story

She's picking grapes
from the groaning vine,
bending low to pull
the bunches drooping
under red and yellow leaves.
Her basket's full, but
she's left the best till last.
Frosted and plump,
they'll make
the sweetest wine.

Her man looks on,
grimfaced,
moustache twitching,
stick working away,
pummelling the grapes
in his possing-tub,
red, white, green,
all mixed up together.
He's no time
for fol-de-rols.

She used to be known
for her ice-wine.
Now she knows that look,
has felt that stick.
She knows the effect of
these beautiful fruits
will be kicks and blows
and vile oaths,
disgusting assaults
on her person.

But what can she do?
She dreads this time of year.
Every chore well done
from harvesting
in the beauty of the late sun
to bottling
in the cool of the cave
is wasted on Mister,
pissed away
down his reeking breeks,
another rod
for her aching back.

Inspired by a painting by Ivan Generalic, Croatian naive painter.

Grounded

I used to be a migratory bird
flying from one little island to another
every year, usually in the late spring.

But it's gone now, that life, will
never come again, I'm grounded here
in the little island that never felt like home.

And how I miss my other home
when I wake up in the morning
in my too small house, my narrow life,

and look out at my three small trees
and think of a wilderness of pines
stretching on up behind me to the Arctic.

The metal herons who grace my garden
will never fly past the headland, or
use their stealth to spear a fish,

camas won't grow here in lakes of blue
and bluebell woods are not the same.
Here, wild flowers give way to farming.

Herne Bay's arcades and pebbles can't compete
with miles and miles of untamed beach
peopled by ancestors and totem poles.

My wings are heavy now and sore,
my back broken, my song a faint lament,
my companion of the spring long dead.
It's all unreachable silence now.

Bobble Tree

She's not been right. I heard her, Christmas-time,
coming down the garden right to our end,
crying fit to bust, bless her. Stood looking at me,
not seeing. I thought, I know, she needs
a bit of a show. I started in the early spring.
Put on a spurt, surprised myself, spread myself
wide as wide, and up and up, lovely stretch,
did me good. She kept coming down each day.
The weather was off, well, you know
all about that, Birch, don't you? You lost a lot
off your top on account of that high wind.
Still, more comfy now, yeah? That haircut!
Beautiful, you look beautiful these days, pet.

I started early because of this weather change.
First my bobbles coming out green, she had
to look hard to see them in my leaves, I keep
them safe when young. Then, a bit too fast
for my liking, out they popped all white,
like lights on a Christmas tree or bobbles on
hundreds of hats. Did me proud, they did,
all my babies. How they made her smile!
It warmed your heart to see her happy face,
because she's not been right. I don't think
she'll ever be right again. I kept on going,
as long as I could, longer than most years,
but in the end, like every year, they had to go.

We're quiet-like, summer time, too hot
to do anything. She stopped coming every day
and I knew she was a bit off, so I had time
to think. What will she feel like come
October, with the garden going into winter
and everything bleaker? She won't want that.
She'll need something to cheer her up.
I've never done it before, no need,
but this year, late summer, so unseasonably
hot and dry, I turned them pink – not bobbles,
they were long gone, but leaves.
She brought him that does the garden to see.

He never notices on his own, daft beggar.
She's hobbling a bit now, stiff, sore I expect,
her face all wrinkled, sheet-white mornings,
so I thought: 'it's not enough. Come on, old girl.
She likes colour, you give her colour'.
And all September, October, I went from pink
to russet to flame to deepest red. Oh my goodness,
what a show! Fireworks on a tree! I was lucky,
mind, not too much wind, just enough rain.
Well, some days she could still do ecstatic,
like she did for the nasturtiums, or the
passion vine, and I couldn't help but think
it's a good old life, is this, to be a tree.

Something is Off

Something is off. My field
is covered in green shoots,
appearing since the harvest,
with patches of what looks like rust,
some kind of chemical, I suppose.
Nothing feels natural.
Like the change in me,
not a gentle season, all things
fruitful in their time, but
a harsh sudden rot,
a greening out of season.

Still Life With Vanitas

How many hairs I've left in the bath.
These damn pills, leaving me sweaty
and faint most of the day, tossing
and turning all night, aching and stiff,
walking like an old crone.

Each hair counting another day
closer to death. All these losses,
these symptoms will only stop
when there's no more oestrogen.
Hair's such a small thing to grieve,
but vanity remains to the end.

We go for a bus trip from Kendal
to Keswick, it's too rainy and cold
for a boat-trip on a lake. Gazing
out the window on clouds and wet
sheep, I catch sight of a huge,
moss-covered oak, canopy
to a circle of dancing daffodils.

Memories flood in of childhood
visits to this watery world, to
Dove Cottage, Grasmere, Rydal Mount,
of recitals in Sunday School concerts,
of the magic of poems in schoolbooks.

What is hair, and what am I doing,
counting the days left, the dying? When
at this moment I could be counting
the waves on the lake, the buds on the trees,
the birds and the lambs, knowing that
the world I leave will always be
alive with poets and daffodils.

Clurabhig Sonata in a Minor Key

Everything moves in this neighbourhood.
The patterns in the grey water of the loch
change so constantly it's a living thing;
and the runt of a rowan tree out the window
waves and waves like a friend trying
to attract my attention; all the grasses
flowing down the slope to the loch,
green, brown, rusty red, sere yellow,
blow this way and that, nervily gossiping,
no direction to their incessant chat.
Even the delicate wee wild barley stems
at the edge of the grassy ledge tremble,
as if afraid the wind will blow them away,
but they're much tougher than they look.
The light on the hills across the loch
changes every moment as the sun moves
in and out of the scudding clouds.
Birds fly across my view and visitors –
the wagtail, the fieldfares who stripped
the rowan's final berries, the boxing hares,
the otters, the collie dog, all keep their coats on,
only popping in, not stopping.

Only I, sitting here on this sofa, looking out
at the frenzied world, am still, immobilised
by a sadness which never goes away.
Every morning I wake up to it, every day
it slows my steps, binds my arms in inertia.
How I wish to be like the birds in the air,
coasting on a thermal, or the fish in the loch,
instead of blown about this way and that
by the constant winds of life and the living of it.
Even being here at Clurabhig is some sort
of accidental decision made not out of
desire, or need, or sense, but some idea
of peace, or at least the end of argument.
Instead of peace, I find this restless wind,
this anguish blowing me about,
buffeting my senses, bringing tears
to my eyes, unexpected gusts of pain.

I am separated from the outside by
these panes of glass, by the injury
to my foot that stops me from walking,
tethering me this side of the window,
onlooker, not participant.

I must move on, leave everything behind,
as I will leave this place next week, when
time sticks its spurs in me. However much I want
to stay in this moment, I'm not stopping either.
I move on to breakfast, a delicious duck's egg.
Then bath. And on with the motley,
sandals and the socks with a hole cut out
for my toe to poke through, the vest
the sweater the jacket the tights the trousers.
It's cold out there, the wind is Arctic,
hat and gloves already in the car, as is
the shopping list to fill the endless need to eat.
Perhaps today we'll go to the headland
and watch the waves crashing onto the rocks
and the gannets wheeling in the air,
hanging onto our hats and our footholds,
or perhaps we'll be dashing along the
almost empty roads, thinking of traffic
jams and road rage far behind us,
to find a folk museum or standing stones
or ruined remnants of blackhouses,
signs of other folk who've battled with
this harsh master of a landscape, or
we'll look at the news in a cafe, oh lord
the news the news, wind from the rest
of the world buffeting our flimsy island
of table, coffee, cake, or we'll be
crowding into a tourist shop with
a bus-load of irritated others, fingering
the all-too-expensive souvenirs, then
on to chatting and bickering in the car
on the way back to the holiday home,

tired and sad, shutting the curtains
against a sky darkening over the
wind-tossed loch, wishing we'd walked
on the wind-swept beach which today
as every day is too cold, too empty.
We are old and sad and forgot to warm
our slippers at the fire. Even the night
will be swept by dreams, and pains,
and restlessness. These days, inside
or outside, there is no peace anywhere.

Wolf in the Kootenays

I am the wolf, the lone wolf
high in the mountain meadow,
far from my kin.
I bask in the blue air
and breathe in the sweet smell
of the sun-warmed grass.
I breathe out the hot breath
of my wild flesh, and the meadow
and the mountain
and I are one.

I am the wild one,
the lost one, the lone one.
I sing for my sorrows,
for the past and the present,
keep a wake for my pack:
my mother, that she
who dripped venom
in the ear of my father,
the leader, the tyrant,
the He who must be obeyed.

A dirge for my brothers,
my blood kin, my foes,
snarls out of me
in the bleak moonless nights.
Oh, woe to the pack who
turned on me, outcast me.
Cry for the lone wolf,
the she-wolf, the fierce one
who dared to defy Him.
Howl down the desert wind,
the dry bones of my life.

I am a grey wolf,
worn down with sadness,
with the weight of the lone years.
No young ones follow me,
no friends surround me,
no neighbours know me.

My soul cries in the night
for its mate.
Grief lends red tips
of fire to my fur;
my fangs gleam in the starlight
as I sing for the dead days.

I eat and I hunt and I eat
against cold days of winter,
blank white days of winter,
black lonely nights of winter,
when the wind moans
and the ice creaks under my weight,
and the snow shrouds all of life,
as I roam alone and lonely
far from my kin.

In this warm summer day
I pause for a moment
in the here and now;
mountain fades into blue air,
fur blurs into grass as
I rest for a breath,
then I'm gone.

Acknowledgements

Poems reproduced here have previously appeared in:

'Chellow Dene': *How Do You Think The Ladies Ride?*, Bumblebee
Press, 2008.
'The Colour of Water': Shortisted for Second Light Competition,
published in *Artemis* Issue 1, Nov 2008
'I Dream of Mexico': *How Do You Think The Ladies Ride?*,
Bumblebee Press, 2008.
'Somewhere in the Netherlands, Summer 1957': *Strix* Issue 4,
Leeds, UK, August 2018
'I am a Field': *Confluence* 4, Wordsmithery, Medway, UK, June 2017
'Red Rebecca': Second Prize, Poetry Book Society/MsLexia
Women's Poetry Competition, published in *MsLexia* 80, Newcastle
on Tyne, UK, December 2018
'Mystic Beach': *As Above So Below* Issue 1, Writing Your Voice,
December 2018
'Clurabhig Sonata in a Minor Key': *Confluence* 5, Wordsmithery,
Medway UK, December 2017

This book would never have come out of the closet without the
unflagging support of Barry Fentiman-Hall, who rescued me from
hibernation; and without Sam Hall, mentor with a whip on the
Confluence Writer Development course. My undying gratitude to
both of you.

Wordsmithery is a Medway-based independent literary arts organisation which specialises in managing literature events and projects, Literature Development, and publishing.
Our publications are available from:
www.wordsmithery.info

A selection of poetry books by Wordsmithery:

City without a head
ISBN: 978-0-9926853-0-0 Paperback, 156pp, October 2013, £12
Writings by: B Fentiman; S Hall (ed); SM Jenkin; AM Jordan; S March; T Moyle; R Smith. Ink drawings by V Wainwright
A collection of poetry and prose taking the format of an alphabetical index.
'... an exceptionally refreshing and eloquent anthology.'
**** FemaleArts

An assemblance of judicious heretics
ISBN: 978-0-9926853-3-1 Paperback, 100pp, full colour illustrations October 2015, £15
This beautiful illustrated anthology documents a large scale collaborative project from literary and visual artists from Medway and beyond. 32 writers and 35 artists' work is showcased in the book.
'...an important snapshot of what was happening in the Medway literary and arts scene...'

One Man's Trash
by Matt Chamberlain and Spreken
ISBN 978-0-9926853-6-2 Paperback, 44pp, 2017, £8
Poems inspired by mundane photos leads to unexpected beauty. This collaboration between two Kent poets started life as a writing experiment to help escape writers' block.
"Luminous descriptions and gregarious explorations of life's detritus..."

England, my dandelion heart
by Barry Fentiman Hall
978-0-9926853-7-9 Paperback, 68pp, 2018, £10
This debut collection marks the culmination of two and a half years of the poet being lost in England in the time of Dave 'n' Teri. These poems attempt to capture the dandelion heart of the nation. "A bold, daring collection that is both a lament for and a celebration of England, the Medway delta and the poet's Northern roots."

Fire in the head
by SM Jenkin
ISBN 978-0-9926853-9-3 Paperback, 48pp, 2018, £10
In the debut poetry collection, SM Jenkin gives us a Blakean book of fire and magic. "You can taste the tang of the Medway in these sharp, observant poems, where myth and history gang-up on the present to tell new tales."